Galoshes

Ga**loshes**

NEW AND SELECTED POEMS

Elizabeth Boquet

Hepzibah Press
Lausanne, Switzerland

Oct. 26 '20

Dearest Marge,
    Thank you for all
your encouraging words!
I miss you, my
birthday partner! Sending
                    you my
                    very best
                    wishes and
    loads of love,

            Elizabeth

(Eve Joanne Hamblett Cassatt's
                    daughter)

For my gallant galosh, Jean-François, who
keeps me snug when the rains fall, takes my hand
and jumps into puddles with me — even the muddy ones.

galosh ga-losh' (noun): a shoe or slipper worn over another in wet weather

Chambers's Twentieth Century Dictionary

Contents

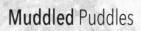

Muddled Puddles

State of Grace

It's a bit like

that moment when you're asleep but realize someone is
on the fire-escape trying to open your window
and you hear them freeze just before they jump off and run away

or when

your due date has passed and, while setting the table, your back muscles
decide to rise and finger their way forward, 'round your ribs and
grip each other over your belly for that first whopping contraction,

or like that dripping August afternoon

in West Virginia when you were sweating out a game of checkers
on the front porch with Grandpa and you saw a way to beat him,
but couldn't stand the thought of him losing so you goofed on purpose.

Yes, it's like that, only this time, when it hits you,

it lowers your shoulders and drops your head because you've been up
all night sorting out fifty years of stuff from your parents' basement and you remember
where you hid that purple starred sparkly marble from your brother after that fight

and you know exactly what to do ⌒

you make your way to the freezer's open door, fingertip the old metal ice cube tray
still on the top shelf to the far left where it's always been and you feel for it ⌒
tangible proof that the past can become forgivably present

and you clasp that last bit of that smooth rounded past

in the palm of your hand and head for the stairs leading to the kitchen
where you know your brother is sitting in his old spot at the table
just staring into his old bowl of cold oatmeal he'll never eat and
you plop that marble right into the thick of it.

Mother Daughter Tankas

Mother to Daughter: Tanka poem to me from my mother,
Eve Joanne Linger Hamblett Cassatt, 2009

To Faraway Child at Christmas
Grandfather clock strikes
dinging through the silent house.
Faraway Child, know
in my heart I hold you closer,
perhaps, than when you were here.

Daughter to Mother: Tanka answer from me to my mother
after her sudden death in a car accident, 2010

To Mother from my Garden in May
This morning, Mother,
I caught you hiding in my
white lilac bushes
slowly breathed in your absence.
Dewdrops trickled down my cheeks.

Reverse Musical Chairs

Sundays at noon
for years
at my mother's table with eight chairs
the seven of us sat.
We'd take our usual seats
and there was always room
for another.

That winter
the six of us struggled
to find our spots at the same table
among the eight original chairs
despite my father's permanent absence
leaving room for two.

This afternoon
the eight chairs remain
waiting round the same table.
There are only five of us left.
We search in desperation
but my mother took the music with her;
no one can find a seat.

Strawberry Jam

What if your sister told you
that the strawberry jam
you were about to spread
on your toast
was from the last jar
your mother ever made?

Would you swipe the knife
across your slice and take
a big bite, or tongue-tickle
a little lick?

Maybe you'd stare at the jar
for a bit; lift it to your face,
breathe in
broken memories
of all that picking

before you closed the lid

scooted back your chair
stepped outside into dry autumn air
held that jar, two hands to your chest

made your way, step by step
to your mother's strawberry patch
and tried to bury it
with your bare hands.

Never Returned to Sender

The cupboards look bare, this lockdown morning.
I sit down at the kitchen table to list all that's missing:
eggs, toothpaste, chocolate, gloves — but
my mind wanders back to when my mother would sit me down,
at her kitchen table, to write wish lists for Santa.

She'd sit with me, ask for details, help with my spelling,
nod her head and smile with me at my wildest dreams.
Sometimes, it took a while — like that year I wished for my own
dance studio in the basement, complete with a ballet bar, mirrors, and,
while we were at it, a percussionist, p-e-r-c-u-s-s-i-o-n-i-s-t.

When I finished, she handed me an envelope and told me to guess
Santa's address — that I couldn't go wrong.
I never did find a percussionist in the basement but I learned to believe
that whatever I could imagine was right. After all, I had proof:
my letters to Santa were never returned.

Said Unsaid

I had a hunch
that one morning
I'd find her alone
ready for a talk, seated
at the kitchen table
with two cups of coffee.

Come sit with me a moment.
Sure, Mom.

I like to think
that she would have leaned in
that I would have leaned in
that we would have spoken
softly together
for as long as it took.

That after all was sipped
and said and heard, I might have
scooted back my chair
rounded the table
squeezed her shoulders, and
whispered into her hair,

I know, Mom. I've always known.
Nothing's changed. I love you so!

But what really happened was
countless mornings
I came down to breakfast
found her alone
at the kitchen table
sipping her coffee.

Our words would slip away
into the day, and
that day into the next
until she disappeared, leaving
finite coffee rings only
on her side of the table.

I hear my daughter upstairs
getting ready for the day.
The kettle is on.
We'll have tea for two.

Geneva Literary Prize, Second Place, 2017. "A clear, deeply felt poem in which memory of a mother and child's ongoing disconnection now impact the child, mother herself, and her own child. Perfect, strong ending." Naomi Shihab Nye

Clearing Mom's Closet

I pull your lipstick
out of that camel coat
you used to throw on
last minute

to be presentable
as you'd head out the door
for errands
in town.

I rub its nub
across my lips
in front of
the hallway mirror

and you looked back
right at me.
I slip on your coat,
Well hello.

There you are!
your lips say
before they settle
into your grin.

Inheritance

The moment has come to sort out what our mother left.
Mine, yours, ours ⟜ are still one and the same ⟜ hers.

We shuffle our wants and deal the rest:
Mine   devotion to serendipity
Yours   the value of volunteering
Mine   a love of poetry
Yours   a smile that knocks off socks

Her deck seems infinite
but we stay
and play until we tie.

Ours   her loss

Constant Companion

By a playmate's open coffin, we first met when I was eight.
Grief surprised me with a boost — for a peek
so I could move on for the others.

Over the years, he'd reappear with the loss of lovers, family and friends.
Our paths began to lengthen and cross so often that,
one day he just hopped on, piggy-back, and never got off.

At home, we let the phone ring and play "Guess who it *cannot* be."
Grief always wins. Last time he got extra points
for remembering my stillborn little sister.

On errands, he rides shotgun. I buckle him up.
We sing camp songs, just like back then with girlfriends from the before time.
We honor Dear Ones at solitary roadside trees.

Grief likes it best when we're on the water afloat on loved ones' ashes.
Rays of fuchsia-peach sunsets are intensified by his insight
of how my mother would match perfectly in her plaid skort.

Birthright

Back then, back there —— as a child in the summer
on month-long sails with my mother
down the coast of Maine, we'd gaze east,
as far as our eyes could see, across the Atlantic.

Hey, Mom! I think I see France! or maybe . . . Portugal?
Oh my! Pass the binoculars! Let's see!

She'd let me believe each island from Kittery Point
to Penobscot Bay might be uninhabited, just waiting
for exploration —— or the discovery of a new welcoming land.
She let me practice possibilities.

What do you suppose they do for fun there?
I wonder what they'll have for supper tonight?

So, in my teens, when I finally made it all the way
across the Atlantic to study in France, it was a matter of course
to fit right in with a new world and its inhabitants ——
who, after all, had just been waiting for me to come and join them.

Bonjour, Mademoiselle. Comment allez-vous?
Très, très bien, Monsieur. Merci. Et vous?

Unsure where I am most foreign in the eyes of others ——
there, back home —— or here, in this life abroad without birthright,
I know I belong because of summer mornings
along Portuguese and French shorelines.

I still connect by looking as far west as my eyes can see
towards those Atlantic islands, grateful liquid bridges never burn.

Carrying the Ashes

for Nanci Hamblett Wilson

You know the granite chunks on the beach,
the ones you see from the dinghy,
the ones that wend their way to the path?
And you know how if you follow the path
up the steepest part of the slope
and climb up into the woods you might
have to grab hold of saplings until
you come to the raspberry patches, picked over
by each of us every summer
right under the grove of tall pine, dripping now
with grandfather's beard?
And farther on, you know how the path
twists to the left and narrows between juniper
and if you go beyond that you arrive
in the clearing with the long stone ridge
bordered by the small field
followed by the big field that tumbles
right back down to the sea, just to the left of the cabin
where there was the singular chair?
That's a fine place to stop
and catch your breath.

Of course, the journey's best done with
your hands free. But you know when
you have a load to carry and your hands are so full
you can't even grasp a sapling?
Just remember that the beginning of the path
is the steepest and, with each step,
the raspberries are getting closer.
And it helps if you have someone
to chat with when you take breaks
and can switch the load from one to the other
up the path to the singular chair.

So, let me know before you set out next time.
I'll row the dinghy and you can put your hand
on my shoulder as we cross the granite chunks.
Bring a bowl for the raspberry patch
and I'll bring an old blanket
and we'll nibble away an afternoon
where there the singular chair once sat
and catch our breath.

Warm Spots

my children leave for school

on their duvets remain

their warm spots

I cannot shake loose

Four and Fourteen

I can see my little boy
squatting in his sandbox
with pine cone people
guarding stick forts
for an afternoon
in the shade
or
feeding chickadees
or
watching squirrels race
along the picket fence
that keeps out.

I see him ⌒ now ⌒
hunched on red sofa
with game console in hand
splattering bodies of blood
for an afternoon
in the dark
and
feeding on ugliness
and
the chickadees go hungry
while squirrels race
along the picket fence
with slats missing.

The Clean Plate

You just grew up.
Just like that.
Just now, sitting at the table
while I had my back turned
to stir the stew.
Just gobbled down all your crusts
as if it were the most natural thing in the world.

I cannot believe
you ate all the crusts, already.

If I'd seen this moment coming
yesterday, at breakfast, when
they were still inedible and evil,
I'd have saved those last crusts
with your little teeth marks, shellacked them
and glued a picture of you, right then, in the middle.

The Search

My daughter hadn't come home.
My daughter was missing.

After I'd searched every face, every place, every who-what-where-when-how,
I searched within.

I didn't blame God; I knew I needed God on my side.
We'd been out of touch for decades.

I prayed. I promised.
I bargained. I listened.

When I looked again, there she was, sitting on the steps of the music conservatory,
just sitting and waiting,

watching over all,
wondering what had taken me so long.

Tearing Down the Tree House

The worst thing was
not being able
to turn away.

If only
the lumberjack could have
left the tree intact.

Down came the house
with the tree
in a back-breaking CRACK!

We couldn't help but look at
its private parts,
its tippy top — normally,

in the deep shade of waving leaves
reserved for birds —
splayed.

Elegy for the Prisoners in My Study

To get to my desk, I shuffle across parquet
made of pine trees who once swayed their days away
in faraway forests before they were stripped
naked, sliced up and slapped with varnish.

To sit at my desk, I plunk into a wicker chair
whose reeds once shilly-shallied in the breeze
somewhere balmy before they were ripped up and
water-boarded until they'd conform into appropriate shape.

To write on my desk, my *glass* desk, sand stretched
some sunny expanse tickled by wild waves before
it was kidnapped and cremated into transparent
flatness on which I put pencil to paper. Paper. Pencil. More trees . . .

I've taken many prisoners to create poetry.
May the trees, and reeds, and sand forgive me.
May I honor them each time I forge my way through
this forest to sit by the shore in the reeds and write.

How to Burn Your Journals

Walk through wettish woods.
Play pick-up-sticks.
Build a pyre with your finds.
Walk away.
Find a spear.

Walk back and strike that match you packed.
Fire!
Sit back. Unpack journals into stacks.
Open marshmallows, spear a few.

Refrain until a blue flame
asks you to frisbee-flick one journal
right into the thick of it. Right into the thick of it
stick one marshmallowed spear.
One journal, one spear . . .

One journal. One spear
to spin what was sticky into sweet.
Let the rest burn bitter black, vanish into ash.
Lick back what you wish.
There are no clean plates.

Chemo-thera-trees

As I walk among them
I wonder
if did they really think
they're keeping it a secret.

It's awkward, knowing.
Just where am I to look?
Up into their bareness?
Down at their waste?

Or, ignore them completely,
look straight on
into the future
which excludes them?

Leaf clumps cling to my boots,
force their rot on me
in vain; I can take them
nowhere.

Fall has failed, once again,
to find a cure for winter.

Hide and Seek at the Bataclan

Paris, November 13, 2015

The hiders: cheaters with suicide-belted access
to ethereal hiding places ⌒ traceless
but for grieving faces searching sidewalks.

The seekers: police, army, press corps, beloved
⌒ my son in front of the TV. I try to shove
the new rules into our silent conversation.

The Bataclan echoes, Come out! Come out
wherever you are! but nobody can breakout
from their infinite hiding spots.

Us and them. We're all entangled in
an eternal endgame. Nobody wins.
Together, we're all it.

Uncle Alfred

I sat on the far side of his bench.
He jumped up and bowed, *How do you do.*

I'm Sir Alfred of Pernessy Park.
But you can call me Uncle Alfred.

I'd find him herding squirrels round the park
or in a happy parade, marching and playing

the cymbals with his hands in his shoes.
He'd hypnotize daisies, offer me tea from

acorn caps. Once, I asked him where he slept.
He said, *Curled with pearls in oyster shells.*

He'd put on pollen lipstick, sit perfectly
still on his bench with pursed his lips,

wait for hummingbird kisses.
He always greeted me as the Queen and

bade me fond farewells, as broken-hearted Hamlet.
And, above all, be true to yourself.

That last time, Uncle Alfred offered me
a whistle-bouquet of the longest and thickest

blades of grass he could find that afternoon.
If ever you need your Uncle Alfred, just pick

one to stretch taut between your thumbs,
put your lips together and blow.

Deep in need, I went to his bench this evening,
with the perfect blade for a whistle.

No amount of sound brought him round; the squirrels
shuddered. Humming birds poked at empty acorn caps.

Loss Haiku

The Memorial
wishes liquefied
I pour hope to dull edges
in the wineglasses

sip and slip away
before those remaining still
silent in their urns

The Ashes
next feed unscheduled
loved one's ash nurses the deep
sea grave suckles slow

The Will
payout estimate
final numbers who-gets-what
death in black and white

ash to paper path
nothing ever quite adds up
just indebtedness

The Dream
nights ago I dreamed
you rowed on against the tide
I hope you made it

Dark Days

shudder

up shades
open windows

close shutters

close windows
down shades

shudder

Sleepless

my train of thought
chugs along

the rails of my brain ⌒
skeins of loose silk

Visiting Parents' Ashes, Penobscot Bay

Waves murmur rhythmic prayers.
Buoy bell moans me toward the dinghy at water's edge.

Oarlocks groan at frigid dips but pull Seal Ledge close.

Defenseless but whole, an orphaned urchin, with its pearled
purple cape, graces a granite slab and welcomes me ashore.

Seaweed guards a trove of hidden mermaid treasures ⌒
sea glass pleasured by waves into elated rubies, sapphires, diamonds.

I cannot see them but know they're there.

Loss

Nights must be swayed into.
Slipped under. Drowned in
so I can surface ⸺ face up
to dawn's loyal warning:
another morning without you

The Recruit

I already imagine
how they'll tell me
as you and your 19 years
pull out of the driveway
on your beloved Harley.

It will be an eager recruit
about your age
who comes to the door so
it's good I practice;
it won't be easy on him.

He'll remain on the doorstep
next to the geraniums, strive
to remember what
he's been trained to say.
And I will listen this time.

If he were to witness my
instant diminishment
into the joints of the tiles
he might quit then and there.

It would be better for him
to stand testimony
to my understanding,
to me slapping my forehead saying,
I always feared this day would come.
This must be horrible for you.
Come in. Have some tea.

We'll sit at the kitchen table
and I will listen to whatever
the recruit has to say, grateful
to help him on his way
with a generous ear.

Flying Time

I doubt time flies.One smooth soar just doesn't mesh.
Maybe it's a jump rope
looping for moments
to join in the game.
Between the hops
blossoms burst
stars shoot
souls enter
exit.

Mow Down

I mow a neat row into the green towards
the compost pile.

Clean grass whisks with moist June light
into the black plastic basket that knocks my knees.

I plunge barehanded into the smooth cool cuttings
wiggle my fingers and come up with scoops of innocent
bladed perfume.

My handfuls hover over last night's potato peels
and this morning's coffee grounds.

I give my thanks ⟋— then apologize and beg
forgiveness before lowering them onto
their rotten doom.

My fingertips stay stained for days.

The Rowboat

Somewhere, between the shore and Seal Ledge,
a fog bank rolled in like I'd never seen — or
should I say, like I'd never felt — because
I couldn't see a thing beyond the stern.
There was nothing to do but
come about, head back to shore.

I pulled her round starboard, shouted,
Comin' about! Starboard she goes!
When I figured I'd made my 180,
I backwatered, steadied and took comfort
in the rhythm of oarlock creak
through the bleak wetness seeping.

A swirling current fought each dip and pull.
Once again, out loud for courage, I shouted
Full steam ahead!
Stroke! Stroke! Stroke! . . .
but the oarlocks would hop out of their sockets,
force a stop to plop the oars back in their spots.

It wasn't until I pulled out of the fog bank
and discovered that I'd pulled
right into the clouds that I realized
my sense of direction had gone
horribly wrong. It wasn't some riptide
making the row so laborious;
I'd been rowing uphill! Into the air! And I still was!

Now, I knew many a fool who could
bring a boat to port or starboard ⌒
north, south, east or west ⌒
but nobody I knew of could
row a boat up or down.
This knowledge gave small comfort.

There was nothing to do but continue.
On I rowed. Up, up, up I went,
beyond the clouds through a fuchsia sunset,
beyond the sunset into infinite indigo
in which yellow stars were twinkling.
I chose one for my heading.
You can find me docked there.

Goodnight Bunk

Aboard the 1929 Alden schooner named Blackbird

Goodnight dinghy.
Time to sleep.
Goodnight ocean
oh-so-deep.

Atlantic waves,
rock and coddle.
Seal blanket
tucked in, swaddles.

Goodnight porthole,
out I peek.
Goodnight clock.
Goodnight teak.

Kerosene light,
story time.
Diesel engine
lullaby.

Goodnight Blackbird.
Time to sleep.
Goodnight bunk
of sweet dreams.

Blessing the Birchermüesli

Lockdown, Lausanne, Spring 2020

On holidays and random Sundays,
when we'd all be seated around

the table in the dining room,
rather than in the kitchen, we'd say

some form of grace before a meal.
When it was my mother's turn,

we'd wide-eye each other, brace
in place for her to choke up.

One Thanksgiving, my little brother
sent us into irreverent giggles,

God's neat! Let's eat!
We'd gulp down mouthfuls of

bounty and kinship and love as if
there were no tomorrow — no

tomorrow that could become today.
This morning, for the first time

in decades, at breakfast, over the
birchermüesli, I bowed my head.

Happy Birthday Twice

Lockdown, Lausanne, Spring 2020

You must wash your hands for the amount of time it takes to
sing "Happy Birthday to You" twice, they said. The first time

I tried this, I got stuck at that part when you add the fêted guest's
name in the last refrain … *Happy Birrrthday, dear so and so …*

I didn't want to jinx anyone; here in Switzerland, it's bad luck to
wish someone a happy birthday, if it isn't really their special day.

So, when the time came to add in a name, I just sang the first word
that came to mind … *dear Si-ink!* … The same word, for both rounds.

The second time I tried, I stood before the sink preloaded with two
Covid names … *Happy Birrrth-day, dear Clus-ter! … Ep-i-cen-ter!*

It didn't hit me until my third visit, as I belted out … *dear Pan-dem-ic!*
that my fêted guest, the one to whom I was singing, was the enemy.

Apology to that Woman at the Post Office

Lockdown, Lausanne, Spring 2020

Honest. In the post office, I coughed to clear my throat.
If I were a cat you might have said I had a furball.
I'm so sorry I made you freeze, eyes wide enough to see
your whites, as if I'd pulled a trigger aimed right at you.

I wish I could have told you that I was just clearing my throat.
How could you know?
I'm sorry I made you clutch your coat, throw your letter at me
and run away but, I want you to know,

I mailed your letter, to make up for it as best as I could.
I'm so sorry.

"Hope" is the thing with feathers

with the first line of Emily Dickinson's poem, #314 "Hope"

"Hope" is the thing with feathers ⌒
 That wants to fly away ⌒ But - tethered to the daily paper
 And infused with news ⌒ stays ⌒

 And hops along covid curves ⌒
 And typed tightrope death tolls ⌒
 That aghast the little Bird ⌒
 That cause its claws to curl ⌒

 I've heard it in the darkest night ⌒
 And in its Cage it tears ⌒
 Plucks away its soft duvet ⌒ in wait
 For the thud ⌒ of morning's paper.

Life is Like a Lady Slipper

Before lockdown, did we all really just
walk around, leave our personal chapbooks
(all with the same moral ⎯ life is fragile)
back home napping on dusty bookshelves?
I suppose, in fairness, we did have to
manage to take one step in front of the other
as we headed out of our doors; looking
backwards didn't seem wise, at the time.

I'd forgotten most of my own old tomes,
found while cleaning and sorting away
these Marie Kondo days; only those that
bring back Joy are kept. My favorite is the
one that opens to a black and white photo of
little me plunging into the pond for a swim
all the way across. I've just shouted to Mom,
Oh yes I can! My Red Cross certificate says so!

It tells of my barefoot adventure, deep into
the pines, on the other side of the pond, where
I hide dripping-dry on a rock and spot my first
Lady Slipper. Jaw-dropped, I squat, cradle
the boy-flower in the palm of my hand; I don't
know the world's name for it yet, or that it's
forbidden. I pluck it up for a closer look,
swim back ⎯ grinning with it in my teeth.

Puddle **Play**

Sunflower

Summer's down to a simmer

but still here to savor.

A sole sunflower stands

in the field of funky weeds.

I eye it in the morning.

It eyes me in the evening.

My vase remains empty.

Aurora

At cockcrow, she basks me in her spotlight
acts as if she might stay a while, hides in the sunrise

blushes innocent pink as if she hasn't been up all night
fingering everything — everyone east

as if she'll never head west to scout out
the next best thing under the sun.

Cento on Tinker Creek

Based on *"Pilgrim at Tinker Creek"* by Annie Dillard

go up into the gaps   stalk the gaps   squeak into a gap

in the soil, turn   unlock more than a maple   a universe

     spend the afternoon   you can't take it with you

point is   not only does time fly and do we die, but

to know it

making hay   should be making whoopee

     raising tomatoes   should be raising Cain and Lazarus

ringing   whole life   a bell

live for it   for the moment   the universe   extravagances

whole show   on fire from the word go

whole world   sparks and flames

we are freaks   world is fine

in the present examine all things   intensely

relentlessly   know you're alive   take   huge   steps

feel   planet's roundness arc between your feet   beauty bats and shines

the present   freely given canvas

creek runs on all night   new every minute

swaddling band of darkness

choir proper praise   nature will try anything once

let us all go have lobotomies   restore us to a natural state

leave library   go back to the creek   lobotomized

live on its banks   untroubled   as any muskrat or reed

you first

Socks

My family's socks seem quite unaware
that they were designed to remain in pairs.
Leftover socks when the laundry is done ⌒
one . . . two! two! one . . . two? Oh no. Just one.

Easter Weekend with Misses Lily & Primrose

Miss Lily, bright delight ⌒
a golden star divine ⌒
sparkles in the sun's spotlight
and makes my garden shine.

Miss Primrose, in her shadow
sits just a little jealous ⌒
wistful for the meadow
flowers' colors far less zealous.

She's the pastel dusk ⌒
to Lily's tawny dawn ⌒
and fades into the night unplucked
stuck there upon my lawn.

With Easter comes the time to pick
which one for my bouquet ⌒
Miss Primrose, sweet but anaemic
or Miss Lily, for a spray.

In the end, neither's amassed.
Not knowing what to do ⌒
I spread a blanket on the grass
and picnic with the two.

Bells, Morning to Night, Bells

morning
bell rings wedding
sledding sleigh bells
school bells   death knells
on cows   on goats
buoys for boats
on time   on toes
wall street   at close
doorbell (not knocks)
Ali wins box
hand-bell choir
call to prayer
help on   the way
sound of the *Guet**
ice cream truck thrum
the Queen summons
clocks chime   tell time
signal lunchtime
wartime   peacetime
time for bed   time
goodnight

*Fun fact: from 10:00 PM to 2:00 AM, Lausanne's night watchman—the Guet (pronounced "gay") (yes, really)—dons his black cape and cap in the belfry of the cathedral, rings the enormous bells and calls out the time before adding, "All is well!" (Sigh) The tradition has been going on for over 700 years.

What am I? (other than a kenning)

Lung-food provider
Soufflé-riser
Fire-eater

Paint-dryer
Goosebump-giver
Sail-plumper

Mountaintop-greeter
Closed room freshener
Plane-comforter

Perfume-passer
Music-carrier
Sunshine-container

Hot, I'm a balloon-filler and sweat-maker.
Cold, I'm a snowflake-maker and Jack Frost's friend.

What am I?

(I am air.)
(And a kenning.)

Abecedarian

Written with the help of my children, Olivia and Alex, on a road trip to Belgium

This may sound strange but just what would you do
if you walked in the door and discovered a zoo?
This happened chez nous while we were away
driving 'round Belgium on countless highways.

We sat in the driveway and we all wondered why
the house looked so different; All were tongue-tied.
"Why all the noises? The lights are all on!
Something has very most surely gone wrong!"
I climbed on the bench for a peek inside . . .
You can't imagine. Just give it a try!
I will describe, now, one sight at a time
what we all saw (but not in rhyme):

Actual anteaters aspirating alfalfa sprouts
Bouncing baboons buttering bananas
Crocodiles chewing caramels continuously
Dehydrated donkeys drinking daiquiris
Egalitarian eagles egging everyone
Flamingos flouring flopping fish
Greedy gorillas gobbling grapes
Happy hyenas heaving honey
Iconic iguanas icing ice cream

Jaguars juggling jellies

Keen kangaroos kicking kiwis

Leopards licking liquorice ladders

Mad monkeys munching maggoty mangos

Nifty newts nibbling nuts

Orang-utans overtly opening Oreos

Proper porcupines picking pickles

Quivering quails quacking-up quinoa

Roman rhinos revelling in ravioli

Sleepy sloths supping sushi

Tigers teething on T-bones

Uakari unsettling upside-down cakes

Vultures eviscerating vanilla beans

Walruses watering waffles with wine

X-ray tetras exhaling xeres

Yaks yodelling "Yummy yam yogurt, yoohoooo!"

Zebras zapping zucchini ziti

Do you believe me? Just what would you do
if you walked in the door and discovered a zoo?

Before You Go

A poem written pre-empty nest

Dearest Olivia and Alex,

There will be mornings that come really quick
but stay-in-bed-laying is just for the sick.
Alarms stop ringing when thrown on the floor.
You'll have to wake up and to get out the door.

Piles of laundry can grow really high
and soon you will understand the reason why.
Sort out all whites and wash them on HOT.
Other things bright: temperature = naught.

Be kind to the neighbors and keep the place nice.
They'll ask for favors; don't make them ask twice.
When left with just crumbs and the odd crunchy dropping,
you might want to eat . . . this involves shopping.

Do take out the trash; find out the right day.
Watch that your cash is not whittled away.
I guess I am through. Just know I love you
and, truly, I know you know just what to do.

Oodles of love,

Mom

Three Ways of Looking at the Partridge in a Pear Tree

I

Pretty little partridge
stuck up in the tree
bit the hunter's cartridge
happy to be free.

II

patient partridge
perched on pear prong
peers at pipers piping

III

There once was a partridge — a bird,
who found Christmas rather absurd.
It sat on a branch,
not to sing or to dance,
but only to splat big fat turds.

Pocket Watch

Who let the pocket watch stop being a thing? I want names!
I bet it was Old Scrooge, by candlelight, a winter's night,
hunched over that dusty desk of his in the counting-house:

one minute drags after the next as his meticulous plume
ticks down row after row of figures, until Ebenezer yanks
the chain dangling from his waistcoat and cries,

Bloody pocket watch stuck in me pocket AGAIN! Bah!
Such a fuss just to tell the bloody time! 'Tis aptly named,
I'll give it that . . . so in my pocket, shall it remain. Humbug!

No, I may not know who, exactly, stopped the pocket watch
but, surely, they never took the time to look within, listen to its
beating pulse, hourly offerings, steadfast minutes, last seconds.

It had to be someone who never kissed mortality's lips, when
time itself becomes the ultimate luxury. No, I may not know who,
exactly, let the pocket watch stop, but I have no doubt that he

ran on automatic, was battery operated by nature, and blindly bided
his time . . . until it all ran out. No, I do not know who stopped
the pocket watch and, on second thought, I hope I never do.

Bah!

Conjugating Our Son

It's almost noon and our son is still
in the third person singular
sleeping alone, in his room, with the door closed.
I think he's supposed to be

in the third person plural
somewhere, with his friends, right now.
I'm full stop. Right in front of his door.
Yes? Non? Oui? Better not. Peut-être but. Hmmm

Knuckles rise to knock, lower to hip, back up to knock.
It's not easy being a first person singular mom
at such moments.
I wish I were in the first person plural with you;

we'd figure out what to do. It's imperative
we teach him how to conjugate
his pleasure with his commitments.
Just how, right now, remains interrogative.

Le Baignoire

Immergée
dans ce flirt liquide,
je me demande
qui est en qui.

Le Lampadaire

Du trottoir,
à travers mon jardin
à travers ma fenêtre
à travers ma chambre
le voleur de la voûte étoilée
vient jusqu'à mon lit me voler le sommeil.

Le Crayon

un crayon

      pour écrire une liste d'objets activants.

une enveloppe

      au dos je peux écrire en français une liste d'objets activants

      avec un crayon bleu.

une chaise

      en osier, celle que je préférais quand j'allaitais, où je suis

      à l`aise pour écrire une liste française d'objets activants

      sur le dos d'une vieille enveloppe, avec un crayon bleu

      que j'ai rapporté du bureau de ma mère où,

      avec les meilleures intentions, elle écrivait

      ses éternelles listes de courses et ses poèmes.

un bureau

      où je m'assieds, à l'aise dans la chaise en osier où

      j'allaitais mon fils, où ma mère m'allaitait,

      pour écrire en français ma liste d'objets activants

      avec son crayon bleu du bout duquel j'espère va sortir

      un poème aussi doux qu'essentiel et pareil à du lait maternel

      avant que j'affronte ma liste de courses éternelles

      je ne les ferai jamais, exactement comme elle.

Trois petits poèmes de la table d'écriture de Caux, France

A Postcard, In Retrospect

Dear Memory,

Wish you were here but you deserve a good break; I work you hard, these middle-aged days. Hope I didn't scare you away with my frequent trips to the laundry room for no apparent reason. Still no sign of my keys or glasses. Hope you come back soon. Before I forget, could you please remember to remind me how Aunt Avis made that salt-rising bread, and if that Chevy on the farm was navy, or more of a royal blue? Cannot seem to color in those simple black and white summer times at Grandma's anymore; when I try, my thoughts flutter-scatter, like all those moths on her back porch, come nightfall, until she'd shut off the spotlight so we could better see the lightning bugs. Maybe you, like those moths ⌒ and, probably, the poor lightning bugs ⌒ prefer to keep to yourself at night? But the occasional spotlight is irresistible, isn't it? I get it. Just come back by morning, please. I'll leave the light off.

Elizabeth

I Cannot Tell

I cannot tell the difference
between my grandparents.

I've never seen them apart.
I've never seen them argue.

They've had 65 years
to work everything out.

Neither one will vacuum or iron
but both are happy to cook and dust.

They talk at the same time
and repeat the same stories.

I'm not sure they even know
The difference between them.

They clipper cut each other's hair and
have taken to sporting each other's underwear.

When I arrived with groceries this morning,
I found them in front of the bathroom mirror;

Grandma was shaving her face. Grandpa was
rubbing a nub of her favorite lipstick on his lips.

Maybe they're losing it.
Maybe they're lost in each other.

Or, maybe, this is what Ruth, in the Bible, means by
… and the two shall become one.

Everyday Haiku

swiss snowflakes don't fall
they alight on chosen sites
divine precision

it's a bit like this ⌒
stray thoughts wrap around my brain
squeeze out poetry

cows bow for thick licks
silver frosted field at dawn
grass popsicle treats

lounging on chaise longue
spring's tender warmth envelops
growing going on

spring birds twerp off key
winter's monotone silence
requires tuning

forecast's blunder slipped
mistook rain's claim on the day
mist took advantage

forsythia star
light shooting through the bleakness
make a wish for spring

our liquid lips sipped
each other for that first kiss
we remain unquenched

wishes liquefied
she poured hope to dull edges
in the wineglasses

kitchen wreckage states
last night's sworn testament in
dinner party dregs

Brake, Brake, Brake

Inspired by Lord Tennyson's, "Break, Break, Break" and the commuters who zoom by my house every morning.

Brake, brake, brake!
      For a chat and a snack and a coffee.
What's all the rush and the bustle and fuss?
      You look like a bunch of zombies.

As your whizzing cars go by
      To your jobs O-so-far away,
I wish for you a day by the sea
      And the sight of your children at play.

While your metal ships sail down
      To the bottom of my long hill
I wish you good luck with your busy day
      And hope that it gives you a thrill.

Brake, brake, brake!
On flat black tarmac, O Please!
Stop ⌒ right now ⌒ your wheels from spinning
      For just one moment and breathe!

Acorns

Acorns must be French.
Somewhere inside
their smooth tan skin
capped with little berets
is *de Gaulle* to believe
they are oaks.

Our Heavenly Butter

Our Butter, which tastes of heaven,
Our hips swear you're to blame.
Thy melting-fun
On popcorn done, adds girth
Which doth zippers threaten.

Give us this day our daily bread
To spread you thick, with even passes,
As we forgive clothes for squeezing against us.
And lead us not to refrigeration,
`Cause hard butter is evil.

Waistlines be the victims!
We'll devour all your glory
On whatever whenever

Forever and ever.
Amen.

When to Flip the Bacon

Splat slabs in a row
on flat black hot.

Watch the taut warm up.
Wait. Wait for surges to sizzle.

When fat backs ripple into transparent surges
to and fro, beneath-below, then

and only then, twist and flip
lest they fizzle into a crisp.

Summer Supper Menu

Starter

peach and cherry sunset cocktails
rimmed with slices of fresh silence

Main

skyful of shooting stars with
lucky tails to slurp like spaghetti
plenty of stardust sauce to splatter

Dessert

darkest chocolate sky-pie
to nibble and lick towards infinity
until there's nothing left to do
but roll over into a spoon.

Critique of Critique

"Elizabeth, Your poetry might be improved
  if you could tone it down a bit."

Dear Professor,

 Please accept my infinite gratitude
 for taking eternity to write
 my poetry's death threat.

I read your pansophy while roil-boiling
an egg the size of an overgrown watermelon
about to explode into smithereens
for breakfast.

Of course, I haven't even the slightest
eeny teeny meeny mite of a doubt
that you are spot-on the-nail-on-the-head
as to how I might improve! YESSSSS!!!

On my knees, searching for your feet
to wash, kiss, massage ⌒ whatever! ⌒ as
your most humble student who will do
her damnedest, I sign, yours, forever and ever and ever more,

Elizabeth!

My Writer's Warm-up

A little voice hums
through my morning finger tips.
Sounds of a warm-up
tap dance shamelessly across the keyboard,
help me get in tune, find the day's rhythm
so I can jump into the creation of the day
and belt something out.

Poetry Creation

It's a forever-first
>> snow day
>> timed hall pass to meet your first crush
>> inevitable kiss
> threat of war, war, awareness of horror.

The creation of poetry is a forever first
>> wave you catch body-surfing that skids you right up onto the beach
>> road trip
>> prank phone call
> phone call at 3:30 AM.

It's a forever first
>> conversation in any other language
>> certainty, after giving birth, that your baby is healthy
>> island hop
> dark car park.

It lays the way for forever firsts to
>> appear anywhere anytime
>> in the everyday
>> during the most ordinary moments of
> this wild ride called life.

Itsy's Mystification

mystified Itsy
climbs right up that water spout
every single rain

bit by bitsy bit
she rises despite downpours
welcomes the challenge

faces come what may
day after dark rainy day
lifts herself above

to find clarity
from a different point of view
makes sense of it all

like the poet who
daily puts pen to paper
to find a reason

Dancing in the Moonlight

secret spot
seduces

water's edge
 suckles my toes

        offers luster
     moonshine

moonlit runway
   drifts   shifts

      wetness pulls me into
        onto liquid dance floor

      bottomless
            shameless

               I
            shimmy
       into
            aqueous
      arms

To Switzerland with Love,
from the Watchmaker's Wife

Dear Helvetica,

I think I've finally figured us out. It took long enough!
Three decades, more or less. I know, I know,
you being the quiet type means I have to go first. And I will.
But only because I'm so in love with you.
How'd THAT happen? you wonder.
Well. Since you asked, first of all,
you have the sexiest watchmakers in the world, but there's more:

Because instead of scissors, you gave my kids knitting needles
in Kindergarten to punch along dotted lines so they'd learn
precision, perseverance, and patience.
Because you made them walk to school.
Because you made them come home for lunch.
Because you made them walk back to school.
Because you have people with The Secret whom I can call for free,
and they'll make 32 warts on the sole of a kid's foot disappear.
Just like that.

It took some getting used to, but I've learned to love the peace and quiet,
that Sundays are sacred — no matter what your religion;
thank you for insisting that I NOT mow the lawn, or vacuum,
or shop on Sundays, and for teaching me that naps and watching
the grass grow can be forms of communal prayer.

Because you're the heart of peace processes worldwide
but your citizens can rarely name their president.
You're neutral but have enough bunkers for the whole country
to hunker down if need be. And those army knives rock.
Because you have the only direct democracy — and the creamiest
chocolate — on the planet, and even though over half of you
have guns, shootings are far out of the ordinary.

Did I mention that your watchmakers are the hottest?
Everything keeps on ticking, no matter what, right on time
because of your dashing watchmakers. Good thing, too, since you expect
everyone to be right on time . . . except for cocktails,
for which you're always 15 minutes late, *exactly,* which is only possible
thanks to those clever watchmaking party animals. Right on! Right on!
What I wouldn't do for a blissful kiss from a Swiss Watchmaker!
God, they crack me up. Now, where was I?

Because you're tolerant and inclusive, even though one in four
of your residents is foreign — including me and mine, once upon a time.
Because, although you didn't need me to teach you French,
you asked me to teach you English and taught me how to do it well.
Because I love teaching you English. And thank you for tolerating my French.
You, somehow, manage to communicate despite
having four languages; perhaps that's because you demand respect
from everybody, and for everybody. You even expect the world to know
that CH* stands for Switzerland and that S is for some other country.

You have multicolored carpets of Alpine flowers up there, beneath snowy peaks,
palm trees down here, on the Montreux Riviera, and watchmakers in both
who get me going — keep me going — my time would stop without them.

You're a 5-star country, Switzerland. I get you, I dig you, and am forever
grateful to you for my personal Swiss watchmaker, who learned from you
how to create gloriousness out of each precious beating minute of our lives
we've created within you, and who still really knows
how to   make   me   tick.

With love from the watchmaker's wife,
Elizabeth Boquet

*CH, the abbreviation for Switzerland stands for *Confoederatio Helvetica*

My Dentist, My Hero

Impeccable.
Teeth to toe in bright white,
braced on his immaculate floor
he smiles all the while.

If I could, I would cheer,
> *Who has come to save the day?*
> *Who can take my pain away?*
> *You can! You can! Yay! Yay! Yay!*

but there's a mini-vacuum in my mouth
sucking up any potential dribble.

As compensation, I put a glint in my eyes
to transmit my delight at the sight of him.
He leans in with pure breath, milky sweet like a baby's.
> *This won't hurt a bit. Just relax.*
> *You may feel like a little nap in a minute.*
> *Just let yourself go and open wide.*

His vision fills my world.
I can only stare
then look away, demurely,
from my hero's eyes and pearly whites,
to the right, at the white wall
with all its white whitey night whiteness.
Nighty night whiteness
sleeping on his white cotton sheets.
White nights on smooth cool white cotton sheets
in his bright white immaculate room
on smooth cool white cotton sheets
pearly clean sweet
cotton braced
smooth milky
relaxed
nap

I open wide.

How to Body Surf

One for the money.
Wade belly-button-high into the sea.
Numb to the thrill of the chill.

Two for the show.
Patience now.
Wait for just the right swell;
he may be well offshore and crestless
but he's already spotted you.
You're a marked target and
won't be missed.
Out rolls a liquid dancefloor
just for the two of you.

Three to get ready.
Play hard to get.
Turn your back on his moves and let
that smooth dude come to you.
No peeking!
Stand your ground.
Keep your eyes on the prize:
a spot in the drying sand
out of his reach.
Bend your knees to be ready
to bound when his little ripples
tap your shoulders to ask
for his very last chance
to cavort and dance.

Now Go! Go! GO!
Either glide and ride, or deep dive.
Whichever you choose,
lunge just beyond his embrace.
Do. Not. Let. Him. Catch. You!
If you do, he'll nasty-slap-wrap
right around you, take you down
to the breathless hell
of pebbles and shells where
there will be nothing left to do but
scrape yourself up and
swoosh away his handfuls of sand
from your droopy suit.

LOVE Letters

The **L** offers its lap.

The **O** wraps its arms around you.

The **V** folds you in, like a double-drawbridge raised with you in its nook.

The **E** shaped hinges open and close the oak doors of the château, for you,
    coming and going as you please, in your blindfold.

M'Amour

Delicious   deep joy
yanks itself up and out of me,
stretches and soars beyond belief,
enveloping my slightest distraction.
Nothing could be more pressing,
no one, ever, more
precious than
you

.

Making Love with a Watchmaker

Until that last moment of inertia,
the truth of our round luminous flux
lays within my wish for patinate perpetual gridiron;
we two, locked in a time warp.

The center of oscillation comes
from your wave-train undulations, rolls
along my feather-edge in pendular motion,
leads to gyroscopic absicissa.

Swiss Alps

Ancient glaciers slip down slopes
for a dip in Lake Geneva,
ooze into tubes that
wind up and under Lausanne
to my home for me
to do with as I wish.
With just a twist of my wrist,
I flush them back.

Red sky at night, sailors' delight

The sun bowed down to kiss the sea,
caress it with hot hands.
The waves, embarrassed red-ruby
in turn, swooned on silk sands.

The moon rose up and spied it all,
their secret meant to keep
but chose to tell prim stars who palled
and fell into a heap.

Eventide, discreet and true,
should never pass the lips
of either fallen stars or moons ⌐
just sailors on their ships.

Missing *A Few of My Favorite Things*

Rubbing my eyeballs and picking my nose
were the first things that they said had to go.
My fingertips tips now have nothing to fling.
Delicate etiquette, Covid-19!

Headaches and fever and shortness of breath
are nothing compared to fear of one's death.
These are a few of the frightening things
many now have, thanks to Covid-19.

When the curve falls,
when the toll drops,
when the masks come off,
we will all breathe and we'll dance and we'll sing!
Nobody will sneeze — or cough!

Book stores, museums and all that bar-hopping
are now replaced by the grocery shopping
which has made for some creative cuisine.
Here's my prized meal for Covid-19:

French fries with rosé and chocolate chip cookies
will make you fat, bet on that with the bookies.
These are a few of those forbidden things
to get you through lockdown this Covid spring.

When the curve falls,
when the toll drops,
when the masks come off,
we will all breathe and we'll dance and we'll sing!
Nobody will sneeze — or cough!

A Lockdown Sorta Sonnet

for my niece, Dossie, on lockdown — who actually has four wonderful brothers,
Campbell, Cooper, Wyatt and Tanner

I wish I were a turtle
with my house upon my back.
I'd hide inside my circle
and I'd try to leave no tracks.

I'd sneak up to your window sill
and leave you yummy snacks,
some paint supplies and daffodils,
and books on this and that.

If I could, you know I would —
one day, I surely will.
But in the meantime, do some good
and try to keep your chill.

Brothers have a special way
of driving sisters nuts;
that which they might call horseplay,
is more *PAIN IN THE BUTT!*

So, when they start, pick up your pen
and write Aunt Liz a poem . . . Amen?

Little Waltz, Jean-François?

Waltz with me, pretty please?
Do not fear. Hold me near.
One two three, you and me.
Round and round, in lockdown.

Little waltz. Giggle waltz
round this room full of gloom;
we can grin as we spin
one two three. Nobody

needs to know. Just let go!
Dance with me. Prance with me!
Itty waltz? Bitty waltz?
Why won't you ask me, too?

Waltz with me! Pretty please?
Do not fear. Hold me near.
One two three, you and me.
Beats the blues! I love you.

Acknowledgements

I'm deeply grateful for my most precious galoshes who keep me warm and dry when I puddle jump — my children, Olivia, Alex — and, most of all, to Jean-François for supporting my writing habit.

And to those who have encouraged me, one way or another, to make a splash and publish: (in alphabetical order, ladies first) Angela Candy, Carmen, Cate, Donna, Elisabeth, Eva, Hilary, Hoan, Holly, Hope, Isabelle, Jo Ann, Justine, Jocelyne, Kimberley, Lee, Leslie, Linda, Lynne, Maribeth, Marielle, Mary, Mildred, Nanci, Stephanie, Susan, Terri — Bart, Dan, Jean-Marc, Jud, Mark, Norm, Nye, Olivier, Philippe, Rich, and Robert.

Thank you to the Pernessy Poets, especially Anita, Bettina, Barbara, Cathy, Christopher, Helena, Jane, JoC, Martina, Nancy, Rachel, Romana, and Saffron, whose fingerprints are on many of these poems.

I am also grateful to: Vievee Francis at The Frost Place, Bread Loaf in Sicily, Al Filreis of ModPo, as well as Laura Kasischke, Aracelis Girmay, Carmen Bugan, Joan Murray, Wallis Wilde-Menozzi and Jaime McKendrick for their master classes given at the Geneva Writers' Group.

Especially generous with their time and support have been the fine folks at the English bookstore, BooksBooksBooks, in Lausanne, Switzerland, and Maureen Thorson, founder of National Poetry Writing Month (NaPoWriMo). To the ever inspirational, patient, and creative Sue Niewiarowski of n-design who brought this collection to life — **thank you**!

And to *you,* dear reader, thanks!

Grateful acknowledgment is made to the editors of the following publications where some of the poems in this collection first appeared:

Summer Supper Menu, featured by National Poetry Writing Month (April 2015), *Offshoots 15* (September 2020)

How to Body Surf, Offshoots 15 (September 2020)

Brake, Brake, Brake, and, I Cannot Tell, *Parody Poetry* (2019)

The Recruit, *Eclectica Magazine* (July 2019)

To Switzerland with Love, and, From the Watchmaker's Wife, Talesmag, (June 2019)

Elegy for the Prisoners in My Study, *Havik, The Las Positas College Journal of Arts and Literature* (May 2019)

Birthright, *Snapdragon: A Journal of Art and Healing* (March 2019)

Reverse Musical Chairs, *Stoneboat* (March 2019)

The Clean Plate, *Crab Orchard Review* (October 2019)

Strawberry Jam, *Crab Orchard Review* (October 2019)

Carrying the Ashes, featured by National Poetry Writing Month (April 2018)

Said Unsaid, Naomi Shihab Nye's choice for the Geneva Writers' Literary Prize (2nd place), 2017

Hide and Seek at the Bataclan, The Society of Classical Poets (2017)

State of Grace, *Offshoots 14* (2017)

Four and Fourteen, *Offshoots 12* (2015)

Everyday Haiku, *Everyday Haiku: An Anthology* (2014)

Sunflower, Acorns, and, Mow Down, *Necessary Fiction* (2012)

Mother-Daughter Tankas, *Offshoots 11* (2011)

About the author

Elizabeth Boquet is a Swiss Belgian-American, born in 1963. She'd just like you to know that her last name isn't floral and rhymes with OK. Some people play video games, or the cello. Elizabeth plays poetry and transforms quotidian moments into tender and playful poems.

Her work has appeared in *Crab Orchard Review, Eclectica Magazine, Snapdragon, Stoneboat Literary Journal, Necessary Fiction, Rock & Sling, Offshoots, Everyday Haiku: An Anthology, Havik, The Society of Classical Poets* and in various other literary journals and magazines. Naomi Shihab Nye awarded her a Geneva Writers' Group Literary Prize (2nd place) in 2017, and her poetry has been featured by National Poetry Writing Month twice.

Elizabeth earned a BA at Goucher College and an MA from Middlebury College-Université de Paris X. She teaches English as an Additional Language to adults, translates from French to English, and runs poetry workshops in Lausanne, Switzerland, where she lives with her husband — a watchmaker — near their two grown children.

www.elizabethboquet.com

Printed in Poland
by Amazon Fulfillment
Poland Sp. z o.o., Wrocław

62952834R00061